Go and Live

SUPRIYA SINGH

For more information, email authorsupriyasingh@gmail.com

ISBN: 979-8-88759-559-7 - paperback
ISBN: 979-8-88759-560-3 - ebook
ISBN: 979-8-89109-064-4 - hardcover

Go and Live

Dedication

For my mom, who is brave enough to live alone and gave me the freedom to live a life I want!

Endorsements

'Go and live' ... I felt those words deep inside my heart, and that's my takeaway from this epic memoir! A Mother's Love is a must read. If you are a daughter or son questioning why parents are the way they are, this book is for you. If you are a parent that finds it challenging to affirm and express your deep unconditional love and care for the well-being of your children, this is the perfect gift. It has always been said that a mother loves differently and Supriya has done an exceptional job at expressing that. The words in this book are heartfelt - Go and live despite my hurts, my pain, my mistakes, my personal desires is truly, and authentically a mother's love.

Stacy-Ann Greenwood,

Writer & Sales and Marketing Executive

Contents

Introduction

This is a story of a daughter's love for her mother. Yet not any mother and not just any love. Love coupled with pain. A pain a mother still feels, and a daughter is grateful for her mother's protection and guidance. A daughter, with the blessings of her mother, taking the biggest risk of her life. A daughter's pain and struggles paralleled with lessons from her mother, all the while appreciating her mother's country so much more.

This is the story of a hero! One that does not bear superhuman strength but gives her love for all that she meets. A hero that does not have superpowers or speed yet has patience you can feel. The battle cry of her standing up for what she believes in. It is a superpower itself. To omit judgment. To nurture where nature has always won. Harsh yet honest. She has struggled and become stronger for it. This is a story of a daughter who finds meaning in her mother's struggles to help her face a new world and a world away from home. This is a story about a mother and a daughter. A daughter who has traveled back to her roots psychologically. To discover, understand, and, more than anything, appreciate herself and her mother. Through her own adversities, her mother instills and reflects the most pure love.

Impeccable nature married with her genuine nurturing was tested yet she remained true through her plight. Through that mother's pain, the daughter gained a great appreciation for her mother in her lessons. She passed on her wisdom to better protect her daughter from her own pain. It gives more meaning to the words spoken in the words that hit her heart. A mother's love and bonding only strengthens with time.

It is something she's blind to, and some have taken advantage of, but I see her intention. She has sacrificed and asked her, but of one thing; to go and live. I could just hear her differently when she said, "Go live." One storm passed, and you can see the rainbow. The damage is done; it's time for a new start.

She showed her strength through reliving her traumas to help her daughter and also to make and find peace. A mother, bringing out her best by only wanting to help and wanting the best for her daughter.

Chapter 1
On the Plane

May 31, 2019

Dear Mommy,

I am on the plane. I smell perfume from the passenger next to me, and I can hear a constant cough coming from a couple of rows up. The plane is almost full, and so is my heart. It's cold, and I'm hungry. I knew I should've eaten before. I can't help but be overwhelmed by all that's happening. I'm moving to Canada. To find work, or as you say, a new life for my own self.

You have shown immense love, support, and sacrifice. You have guided me, my siblings, and more. The feeling of the unknown reminds me of your words of faith and trust. I have come to appreciate them so quickly but so strongly. Seeing what you have gone through, yet your faith only became stronger, and your trust in God was never questioned.

You say, "My heart will be at peace when someone has yours." Thank you for setting me free. I know it was hard for you. I want you to know you will always have my heart as I embark on this journey. I'm going to take a nap now, should be in Vancouver soon. I promise I will write.

With love!

–Gudiya

Reflection

Have you ever observed tiny details, like smells associated with people? Write something you remember on your last flight or any sort of travel.

Chapter 2
Leaving the Comfortable

June 2, 2019

Dear Mommy,

The discomfort of leaving the comfortable. I sit in this taxi heading to the airport alone with the smell of you lingering from our last goodbye embrace. The constant whizzing by of people and places gets more and more distant, and I slowly remove myself from her almighty landscape. There is a fear of the unknown. Yet, the love you give for me and all the wisdom you have passed on gives me hope, faith in myself, and trust in the journey ahead.

Behind me, the dark clouds seem to remind me to focus on what is ahead; the sun off in the distance tells me to bask in the now and that brighter days are to come. Just over 1000 years old, Georgetown, Prayagraj, with its parks, castles, colors, smells, and people, will always be in my heart, as will you, Mother. For I feel shame in leaving you, but you have, with your love, reinforced my freedom. My guilt for leaving seems to deflate more, the farther the taxi's wheels go round.

The bumpy road leading to the airport is dirty, windy, and bumpy. Maybe again, symbolic for today, I close the door to the past and focus on the journey I'm about to embark on.

With love,

–Gudiya

Reflection

Write down any experience you had when you did something uncomfortable to gain a long-term benefit. How was your experience?

Chapter 3

Arriving in Canada

June 9, 2019

Dear Mommy,

I have arrived in Canada! It is cold yet colorful. Canada has many different colors than back home. The smells and sounds, sometimes there is quiet in the streets here. My nostrils have been overwhelmed by the foreign smells I'm taking in. The feeling of desolation and desperation wants to creep in, but you have taught me better than to run from such feelings and embrace them.

I think of you, your nature, and your love often. As I am in a new land, my motherland still whispers to me in the wind. Not to come home, but that I'll always have one. You are in my heart, and my heart is where my home is. It is intimidating, but I know that it is all worth it. I am lonely and maybe scared at times, but that is when I realize and appreciate that I am on this path for us.

So many things here remind me of you, Mother. None more than Mother Nature's unforgiving, brutal honesty. As you have lived your life in such a tremendously bold and inspiring way, you have lived your life on your terms. Now I must do the same, as hard as it is. I understand and appreciate how it was even more difficult for you in your time.

From my heart to you, where my heart is.

With love,

–Gudiya

Reflection

Did you visit a different country or an entirely new place different from where you are currently living? How was your experience?

Chapter 4

Difficult Times

August 16, 2019

Dear Mommy,

These are tough times for me, trying to adapt to a new country's social behavior, traditions, and language, feeling overwhelmed by the challenge of finding a job, making friends, and trying to create a healthy and positive balance. I feel a little guilt and anxiety creep in for me, being so many miles away from you. I wish I could be there for you and with you.

As we are miles away, my love and appreciation for you is only intensifying. Yet I remove myself from these temporary hurdles when I think of you. For it is in my pain and adversities that I remember most of your strength, resilience, and persistence, being selfish when needed, but the most giving person I've ever known. I think of seeing and hearing about all that you had to go through, but you choose and have trust and faith in God. Most important, trust in yourself. Nowhere near do my struggles compare to the pain, abuse, neglect, loss, and isolation you must've felt. It could've created a toxic and cancerous ball of resentment, pain, and spite. Yet you rise above your adversities and choose forgiveness, showing love and grace.

You're so strong, even through your father's emotional and physical absence. His not showing love and guidance to his daughter pained you so deeply but also forged a stronger resolve, helping you turn into a more independent and confident woman. Not to mention it was during a time a culture or society did not treat you equally for being a woman.

I think of how, at the age of 10, you were forced to move away from your mom and dad to become a help for your aunt and uncle away from your own home. I could not imagine the feeling of abandonment and betrayal you must've felt. Yet again, you were void of spite, hate, pity, or resentment. You shifted from blame to love, for you knew to trust God's plans despite the pain in your heart. For the greater good of your family, you sacrificed your education and future dreams.

Being forced to marry at 14 years old, at an age you were wise far beyond your years, but you still had to grow into the woman you wanted to be. So, again, sacrificing so much of your freedom and basic adolescence also helped cement your strong foundation. Although you had no support or encouragement, at times, you chose to be all of that for yourself. Yes, at a very young age, to feel the burden and pain; instead, you rose to the occasion, defining the woman, wife, and mother you so greatly became.

You may have married young, but you also divorced your fears and adopted a trust within the universe and God that your children now have as their guide. For that level of faith you have passed on, I thank you from the bottom of my heart. It is that belief that you bestowed that helps me in these times, but I know that where I am now is okay and not forever. The now of where I'm at is leading me to the me I'm becoming and everything I need.

And as long as I have you, I have everything I need. Like a flower, Mother, through the seasons, you have watered me a bounty and tended to me delicately with so much love, and now it is time to let the mother of mothers, Mother Nature, do her part. I trust her. Like an aunty, she is there. Trust.

Trust I love you,

—Gudiya

Reflection

Have you or your parents ever had any life-changing experiences? How has that affected your life positively?

Chapter 5
Rituals & Routines

December 16, 2020

Good morning, Mommy,

It is still dark here. A slight, crisp cold air lingers around my apartment, and it wants to challenge my discipline. As I lay in bed and think of my morning and day ahead, my most powerful thought most mornings is you.

On this particularly cold and wet morning, I can hear cars going by and the odd crow cawing, probably reveling in the excitement of a buffet of worms that come out here in Canada when it rains.

I think of how much I don't want to get up today; then I think of you again. I feel the love pour in and feel inspired to begin my morning routine and rituals. Those that started as a way for you to escape the constant pressures thrust upon you at a young age and give you peace during turbulent, difficult, and lonely times. They were your friends when you were alone, and you had no one. They give you self-discipline

31

and awareness of your psychological and emotional mistreatments and neglect. They give you an endless stream of love, empathy, and creativity, which you pour back into the world abundantly and so authentically.

You have taught me from the age of 4 the true importance of good habits, routines, and rituals. You've shown me the significance of putting out and conserving good energy, and having the wherewithal and awareness of myself, others, and the world around me. I am thankful for all I have and what I do not have. From waking up at 4 a.m. every day, being in tune with Mother Nature and all of her blessings, to being conscious of the birds, their songs, the fresh air hugging your skin, and the radiant colors that help paint how we perceive the world and sometimes just the silence. It all started as an escape from inadequacies, strengthening your resolve and love for yourself. It's a discipline that you put on yourself in a way to distract but evolved into a way to hold yourself accountable to yourself—not letting anyone have that power.

Morning walks are quiet, yet in those moments is when our hearts speak the most. A calm would wash over us as the sun basked upon us. I remember watching you feed the birds and the stray dogs, an act so selfless, so telling of your richness. That angelic and pure smile reminds me, "sometimes there is no need to talk. Just listen." Mother Nature will give you gifts of the moment and speak to you. Born in India, yoga has become a way of expression for centuries of cultures. And some take the true practice for granted. You have instilled in me a deep connection and appreciation to the commitment and practice. You have created a fundamental and natural foundation for yourself through your routines and good habits.

Love,

—Your daughter

Reflection

Is routine important in daily life? What rituals or routines do you have that form the basis of your life's foundations?

Chapter 6

Family

February 17, 2021

Dear Mommy,

You had a very tough childhood, I know, from being sent away at a very young age, not fully understanding, to the void of a father figure in your life. Yet you became the matriarch of our family. You made sure that we had better childhoods with an unwavering love you never faulted. I felt and still feel it. You did so much for us. You became an amazing wife.

Yes, it wasn't easy; I understand as well, but for all that you went through, you made up for it in so many ways. I feel we have a special bond. Everything we have been through together has only hardened our love and strengthened our connection. I hope I can give you what you deserve and be at least half the miraculous woman you are.

It is my wish that I can create the family as you did. Our struggles have made me more aware of what I want. I am constantly reminded of your adversities and what you had to go through. You have a profound effect on me. What you had to go through and the difficulties of your family has made you a stronger, more independent woman. In doing so, you have passed on such wisdom, love, strength, and so much more to your family. I hope I can be that for you and my future kin too. For it is with your hard past, I strive to make a better future for you and our family name.

Love the family and, of course, you, Mommy.

With love,

−*Gudiya*

Reflection

Is family important to you? If you have a toxic family, how do you deal with it?

Chapter 7

March 21, 2021

Dear Mommy,

It starts from something inside of us trying to understand something more on the outside. It isn't *what* you believe, but *how much* you believe in that something. It doesn't have to be religious, but is always spiritual. It is something so very important. It can carry us when we can't carry ourselves. It is something that grows when you water it.

Mine deepened forever more by your love and lessons. It is my faith. Your faith was instilled in you at a very young age; your faith in God. Your faith in yourself. Your faith in your journey, from the pain of loneliness and the lack of direction. You crested a way for yourself to find healing through a spiritual approach, yet with a love for Mother Nature and yourself. You were faced with so much, but you believed it served a purpose for your path. The faith you have also defined by those rituals you have practiced for so many years.

It is a level of discipline you have for everything that restores my faith. It has given me a sense of trust that no one can take from me. The same faith that has been instilled in you is now being infused into my every day. I must have faith and give time to recognize it. It begins with the faith I have in God and myself. My rituals are a way of being with the energy of God and a way I connect to you. More importantly, it is a way that restores my faith.

Love you, Mom,

—Your Gudiya

Reflection

Is it important to have some type of faith? How effectively helpful is it in overcoming difficulties in your own life?

Chapter 8

Forgiveness and Failure

April 6, 2021

Dear Mommy,

I can only fail if I give up, and you, Mommy, have shown me that perseverance is more important than being the best. If I believe in myself, in time, God and the universe will provide as it did for you. You did not question or fight the plan God had for you. You had your downs, such as trying to navigate yourself in a place where you were not accepted. Being aware of not just your failures but others around you to learn from helped shape the resilient woman you are today.

So now, years later, as I take the steps into my unknown, I hold dear the lessons I've had to go through. Every failure is an opportunity. If I'm not failing, I'm not trying hard enough. You have taught me to face my failures with a smile and know my time will come. I have learned so much in my little time here. I must set out and make things happen for myself. It almost comes from a place of peaceful fear to achieve my own definition of success. Here, it is required of me to fail, to make peace with the voice in my head, to keep going until I am happy.

Failure is scary. It has taken years for me to get to this point. I am remembering how truly fragile the mindset is, how delicate and sensitive it is. How easy it is to be consumed and gripped by the feelings of inadequacy. Forgiveness and failure run hand in hand. It is essential for me to be able to forgive others, but, more importantly, myself.

When I do forgive myself, I make it okay to be where I am, and I know that I will get better. Witnessing your willingness to prevail in the face of adversity constantly replenishes my heart when things are difficult. Your difficulties paved a way for me to do what I am doing now, and I won't take that for granted. When I think of the hard times, I think of you, pushing through with that smile and constant assurance that it is okay. Just the thought of you helps transcend my strengths and puts things into perspective. I know it must be hard for me, but I must accept and struggle where I want to struggle.

You have always told me you will always love me, whatever I choose to do. As I work to create the life I dream of a world away, your love inspires me to work harder and to persevere, myself. Whether failing at relationships, jobs, trying to find places to live, making friends, or adjusting to social pressures, I am always loving and learning. It is a way of teaching myself. Through your words, it is helped define me as the strong woman I am striving to be. I cannot and will not fail when I have you, Mommy.

Love you, Mom,

—Your daughter

Reflection

Is there someone you have not forgiven in your life? Is there something in your life for which have not forgiven yourself?

Chapter 9

Break Up

June 19, 2021

Mommy,

It is the same place where I hurt and where I heal. With self-love and your love, the pain is tolerable. As much as it hurts, I show the mental, verbal, emotional, and physical scars proudly and confidently. Sometimes the scars don't need makeup, but really do help you build up.

I have left him for good. He has caused me enough pain. The words cut deep, the bruises hurt to the touch, and I have blamed myself for long enough now. The feelings of inadequacy he thrust upon me because of his ego … now I can see it. The strength in you gave me the courage to leave. It's the true desire for happiness in which all deserve, and I want to make you proud.

I began wrapped up. Also wrapped up in his warped ways: how he treated me, how he didn't treat me. The psychological damage is now like springs, blooming ever more beautiful with my self-worth and confidence, like the sun shining brighter. Where once was darkness and despair, there is light and faith, patience and trust.

You've always reminded me of your love and the importance of self-love. Because of what you endured and the love you had and have for yourself, you have managed to become more at peace. You understand more that suffering is necessary for us to see and fully appreciate who we are and what we really deserve.

With my heart and mind open, I am able to move on with peace, knowing and trusting whatever comes next. Yes, there are moments of hurt, and there will be more, but that's okay. I have faith in it, and it is building me into a strong, independent, and confident woman, as it did you. There is no rush and no pressure. Everything will come at the right time. I can't give up when I have you to look up to.

Love you so much, Mommy,

—Gudiya

Reflection

Have you ever had your heart broken? How have you handled a breakup?

Chapter 10

Strong Foundation, Stronger Women, and Opportunities

September 15, 2021

Hello Mom,

As I become more familiar and comfortable with the West world, I do not take for granted the opportunities you have given me and those I am creating here. None are bigger than you giving me the opportunity to move here and make my dreams a reality. The opportunities here seem so much richer, ever more evident and abundant for women. Why does it seem that our society and culture do not allow the same basic opportunities for its daughters? It has become so much clearer as I fit into life here in the West.

There's such a systematic denial or divide of treatment of women in India. Perhaps even more, a depriving cultural society that, for blindly or more sad, ignorantly deprives her women. All that you went through created a strong foundation. The pillars of adversity affirmed your strength by your choice to choose love and forgiveness. I am forever grateful for I have the choice of education, who I marry, and so much more. In so many ways, it is because of you. With your blessings, you've set me free.

You say that your struggles won't have to be mine, but I will have my own. I understand that more now. All the struggles you went through helped you become the woman you are today and are becoming tomorrow. You've said our struggles are there to help us, perhaps more stepping stones to affirm what and who we want to be. These tests are a way to remain true and awaken a part of our greater selves. The inspiring woman you are will forever help me in the difficult times to choose happiness and love. One stepping stone at a time.

Adversity is there to help show me what I want and what I believe in, and it also gives me the courage to speak it, as does your reinforcement to trust God, the universe, and to have faith. It's the foundation you helped build, a foundation you stand strongly on, affirming by your struggles and lack of certainty in given relationships. Perhaps even more in the privacy of a good culture society. It limits your potential, but only makes the foundation even stronger. It is but being born in a certain time in the same place. You have made sure I do not adhere to such rules, laws, or beliefs.

You were a victim of patriarchal tradition that has been sewn sadly into the Indian cultural fabric for thousands of years. A system was put in place where, society or government, men hold all the power, and women are largely excluded from them. Crippled are some societies' rituals, lost in time when we even understand or head our independence. The generations in our lifetimes have a profound effect on us women. This patriarchal behavior and the society and culture denounces its women as equals or, in the past, as human beings. As for you, Mother, you deserve patience, kindness, and love. Yes, none more important than the love we give to ourselves, but you deserve nothing less; you will have always given more than I will be. You have freed me from such limited beliefs and culture controversial norms.

The dowry, the bride's family bringing property, treasures, or money to her husband at the wedding, the workings of the dowry has evolved from being meant to serve as a means of safeguarding the wife against the real possibility of ill-treatment by her husband and his family. Though still illegal, it is still widely practiced. It creates generations of us by resentment and ego. You and your family did not have the money or anything to give as a dowry. That eventually built a wall, causing division. You do not let it affect your desire to be that amazing wife and mother you've always wanted to be, though not his fault. You were aware. It was maybe both a blessing and a curse in a time that made it only more difficult. Though you know, Mother, you showed love and hugs.

Does love even translate differently when we cross borders? How does one's cultural representation of love differ from another? The first love I've ever had was from you; it was natural. A mother's love. The daughter's love for her mother.

You taught me first to love myself. In doing so, it has brought me here to Vancouver to fight and be that more. The limits mother country has had on you, myself, and you know, I'll be staying here as I look in the file [my Canadian Visa Application] for that long.

You have allowed me to dare to go further than those limits, to seek out the best of myself so I may first love myself but, of course, others authentically and genuinely. I do see your pain, loneliness, and struggles with that. As you're able to love and be honest with yourself for fixing it affected your relationship with him [Dad]. You are blessed or cursed to be aware of what you deserved. On the path was your own love, but you come in from the constant opposite, dealing with it in the darkness, bringing love to your life. Even to rebel against the limit set on you because of what one or cultures believe. I know how hard it was for you to stay true to yourself when said culture conforms us on the most core level.

With Love,

—Your Gudiya

Reflection

How important is education? Do you feel you didn't have that? Have you ever considered exploring other education media rather than the usual ones?

Chapter 11

Death

December 11, 2021

Dear Mommy,

We lost Dad. Yes, he's been suffering for some time from liver cancer and dying for over six months, but knowing never makes it easier. It has been a challenging for me but even more difficult when I think of you. You have been honorably dedicated and given so much. I know your love for him was immeasurable.

Your loyalty, patience, and selflessness are etched in the fabric of your heart for him. There was neglect and abuse. You discovered more of yourself, and you stayed loyal and true. Your self-worth was affirmed by a man who did not fully appreciate you. Was it justified by culture or society? Or a history of systemic behavior? Why is it allowed?

The patriarchal society you were raised in imposed guilt of allowing and perpetuating such a behavior and mindset. Yet there is no blame or hate in your heart. Since ancient times has been tradition, the treatment of women and wives. Why have we evolved so much yet traditions of men arcade? It is us women that give India kings and her sons. You have stood by a man who had no nothing more, to no fault of his own. You have forgiven. When you were hungry, you fed him, when you were thirsty, you gave him water. He didn't know the lesser, you just knew more. So, you loved more, a deeper love. None deeper than the love for yourself.

There's always a new beginning in death. And this is yours: a rebirth. He will always be with you now, at peace, and it's all blessed by God. It's pure love radiating down on you from the heavens.

Seeing your strength through this difficult time inspires me to be the most that I can, to make you and Dad proud, to make myself fulfilled. I want to love myself and be like you, a strong woman who knows what she deserves. Dad is with us in the rain, and when the sun shines. He is with us during the worst and the best of times. He'll be there for the celebrations. He is the reason for having that much more motivation from your morning walks to our 5 p.m. phone calls. He is here with us and reminding us to trust. I'm glad we are here for each other and have Dad in our hearts forever.

Love you, Mommy,

–Gudiya

Reflection

Have you ever had to deal with anyone's death in your family? How did you deal with that experience?

Chapter 12

Conclusion

January 23, 2022

Dear Mommy,

When I think back to when this journey really started, it was so long ago. Long ago, when you gave me the foundation that I have only made stronger and can stand firmly upon. I was just a girl when you started pouring a tendering love and giving the structure to build upon a graceful life. Of course, it comes with pain. I honor you for it, all you've gone through and what you've done for yourself, what you've done for us. What you've done for so many. You have fought back against norms and traditions, facing backlash and being an outcast for it. You know your heart. You lead with your heart. It is genuinely apparent, though it came with suffering. It has come from loss. Yet you have found peace.

Your peace came with loving yourself more and going deeper into the connection of yourself, forgiving those who have hurt you, forgiving your past self, and being accepting that we are beautiful who we are and we're always improving. I know it wasn't easy for you, but you found it in your heart still to put others and us first. You have made a dreamer, a loving, hopeful, and courageous woman out of me. Thank you for your unwavering support and reinforcements.

I'll always cherish our 5 o'clock phone calls, getting your mail, and writing you on the rainy days. And where we've been and where we're going. It is a beautiful place, Mommy. I look upon my days here differently with you in mind. It is as if it beautifies it all, makes the tough tolerable and trustable. All the lessons I have learned and continue from you are immeasurable. It is with your grace through all you have taught me. You remind and show me to put a self-love above all, a love for nature and trust for her ways.

You have strengthened my faith and trust, trusting the unknown, walking into the uncomfortable with a smile and a hug. Between the parallels of our own shared pain, we both have found each other and ourselves. The love I have for you is infinite, as is the wisdom you pass on to find and create a deeper connection in what I am doing. It will always translate into a deeper connection with myself, others, and the world around me. You painfully sacrificed your present; you have given us a better future. There is simply so much to thank you for, but this is just a beginning.

As these past years have been more difficult, it demands me to persevere and be there for others. I want to and will give you more, Mommy. As I am on my path here, my dreams have grown as I have. As I once was gripped by fear, now it is hope. What you have or don't have don't define you, though I have you. You have helped define me. I miss the sounds of the city vendor, the dogs barking, seeing the three rivers every day, your pain, struggles, and everything you have been through, making me better appreciate this path. I want you to know I feel your presence and love during my challenging times. You have shown me the strength of a mother so profoundly.

The next parts of the journey are scary and exciting, but they are just better knowing you're with me. I will make you proud; I promise. As far as a review, Mother, you deserve patience, kindness, and love. Yes, none more important than the love you give to yourself, yet also you deserve so much more—the *more* you were once deprived of. I will make it right and up to you, for God and you have given me that. I'll always have the choice to be more, that more I will be. The more I will give you. Every day. I promise.

Talk to you at 5,

—Gudiya

Reflection

If this book has changed your perspective or given you some new information, please share it with me.

Thank You for Reading
Go and Live!

Loved This Book?

Have you enjoyed the concepts you've learned from my book, or want to learn more? I would love to hear about it! Want to help others find my book? Don't forget to leave a review! Your review matters and it matters a lot! Feedback is always welcomed and will make this and my future books better. Head over to Amazon or wherever you purchased this book to leave an honest review for me.

Thank You!

Let's Connect

Website: www.authorsupriya.com

Email: authorsupriyasingh@gmail.com

Instagram: @supriya.usc

Acknowledgments

I would like to thank my mother, who is bold enough to share such intimate details of life that gave me encouragement so that I can live fearlessly!

Moreover, I am blessed to have wonderful friends like Stacey, who nudged me to rethink again about publishing my book (which I had kept on the back burner due to the busyness of life).

About the Author

Supriya's journey has been throughout India, the United States, and Canada. She works as a Software Engineer and likes to read and write. She has seen a lot in her 35 years, and this book is just a part that she wanted to share with others to give tribute to her mother.

Made in the USA
Middletown, DE
06 October 2023